Room by Room Tissue Box Covers

LEISURE ARTS, INC. • Maumelle, Arkansas

Table of Contents

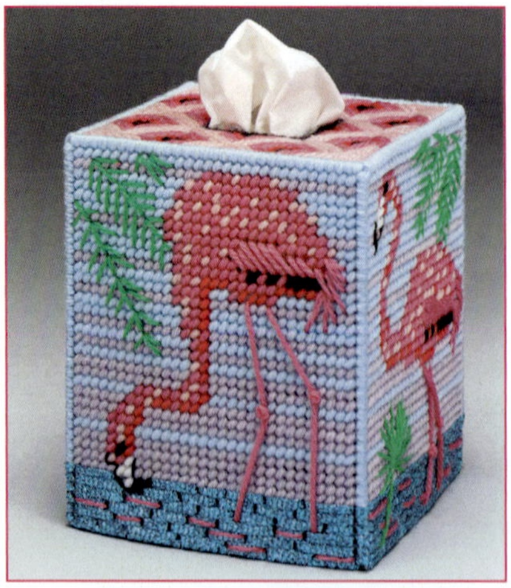

Table of Contents

FORTIES FLAMINGOS

Size: 4 1/2"w x 5 1/2"h x 4 1/2"d
(Fits a 4 1/4"w x 5 1/4"h x 4 1/4"d boutique tissue box.)
Supplies: Worsted weight yarn, Rainbow Gallery metallic blue yarn, and embroidery floss (refer to color key); two 10 1/2" x 13 1/2" sheets of clear 7 mesh plastic canvas; and #16 tapestry needle.
Instructions:
1. Follow charts to cut and stitch tissue box cover pieces, working backstitches and double French knots last.
2. Referring to photo for yarn colors, use overcast stitches to join Sides along long edges. Join Top to Sides.

Top (32 x 32 threads)

KEY

COLOR (YARN)	COLOR (YARN)
white - 1 yd	*pink
lt pink - 10 yds	*green
pink - 17 yds	pink double Fr. knot
lt red - 6 yds	*Use 2 plies of yarn.
purple - 25 yds	
lt blue - 30 yds	COLOR (FLOSS)
black - 3 yds	†black - 1 yd
metallic blue - 9 yds	†Use 6 strands of floss.

Side #1 (32 x 38 threads) (stitch 2)

Side #2 (32 x 38 threads) (stitch 2)

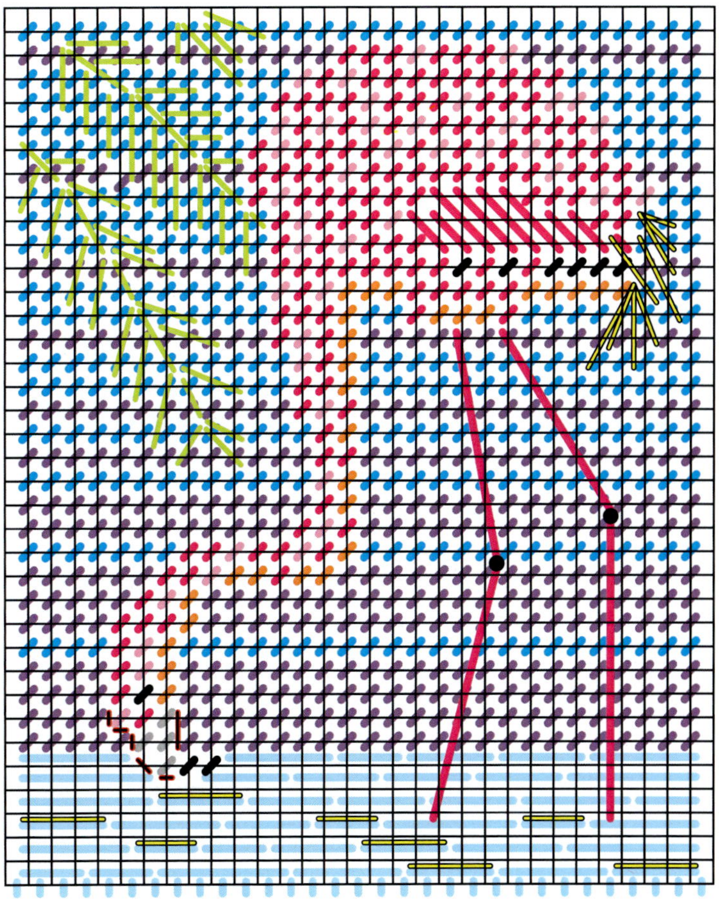

FERNS

Size: 4 1/2"w x 5 1/2"h x 4 1/2"d
(Fits a 4 1/4"w x 5 1/4"h x 4 1/4"d boutique tissue box.)
Supplies: Worsted weight yarn and Paternayan Persian Yarn (refer to color key), two 10 1/2" x 13 1/2" sheets of clear 7 mesh plastic canvas, and #16 tapestry needle.
Instructions:
1. Follow charts to cut and stitch tissue box cover pieces, working backstitches last.
2. Using ecru overcast stitches, join Sides along long edges. Join Top to Sides.

Top (32 x 32 threads)
Complete background with ecru tent stitches as indicated on chart.

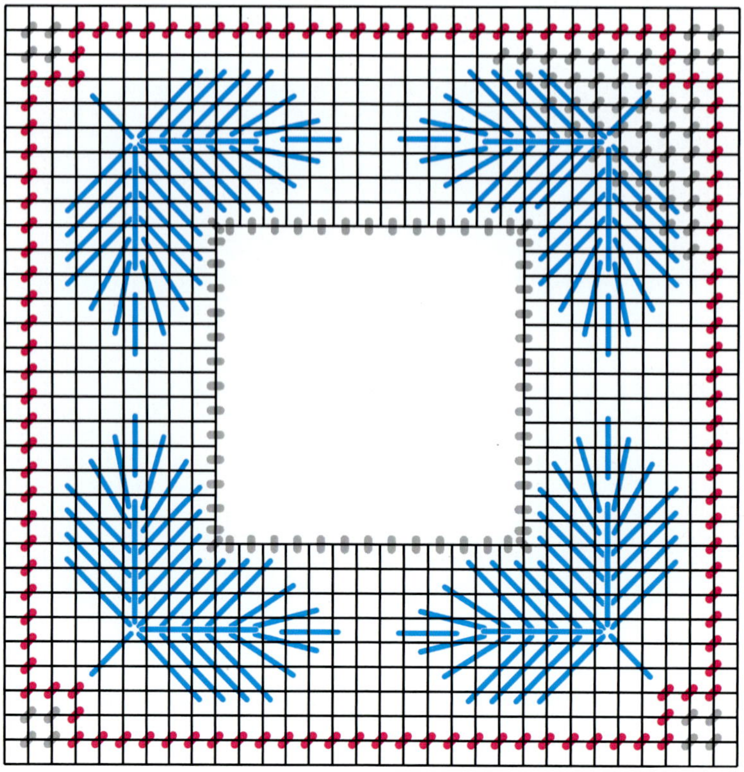

KEY

	COLOR (WORSTED)
▨	ecru - 81 yds
▨	coral - 12 yds
	COLOR (PERSIAN)
▨	lt green (631) - 13 yds
▨	green (630) - 9 yds
▨	dk green (691) - 10 yds

Side #1 (32 x 38 threads) (stitch 2)
Complete background with ecru tent stitches as indicated on chart.

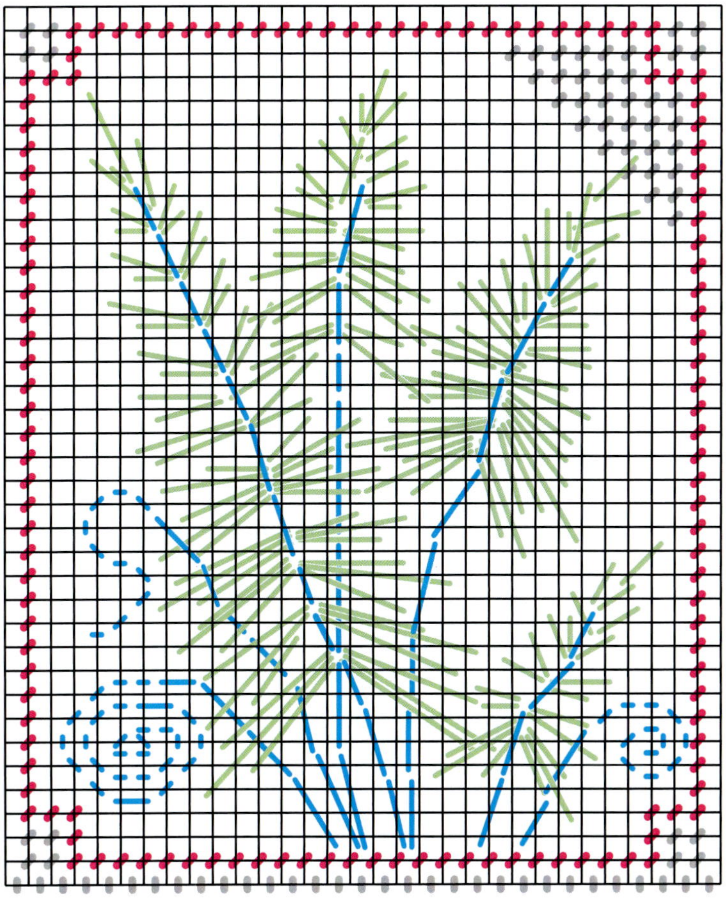

Side #2 (32 x 38 threads) (stitch 2)
Complete background with ecru tent stitches as indicated on chart.

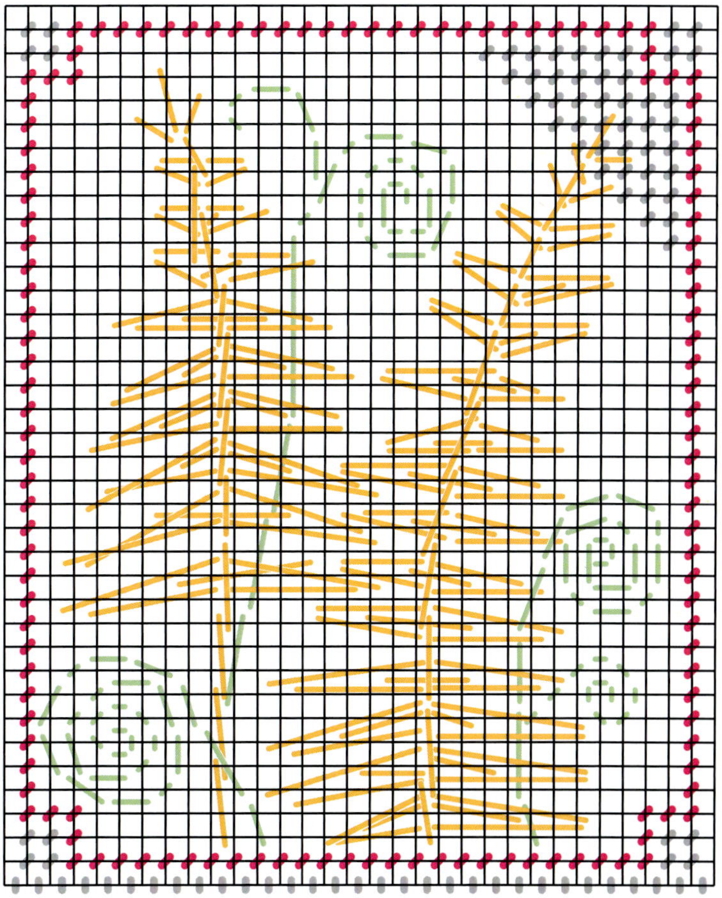

CHICKEN COOP

Size: 4 1/2"w x 5 1/2"h x 4 1/2"d, excluding raffia
(Fits a 4 1/4"w x 5 1/4"h x 4 1/4"d boutique tissue box.)
Supplies: Needloft® Plastic Canvas Yarn and embroidery floss (refer to color key), two 10 1/2" x 13 1/2" sheets of clear 7 mesh plastic canvas, #16 tapestry needle, and raffia.
Instructions:
1. Follow charts to cut and stitch tissue box cover pieces, working backstitches and French knots last.
2. Using brown overcast stitches, join Sides along long edges. Join Top to Sides.
3. For straw, refer to the Diagram and tie 3" lengths of raffia to unworked threads along bottom of tissue box cover. Trim ends of raffia.

Diagram

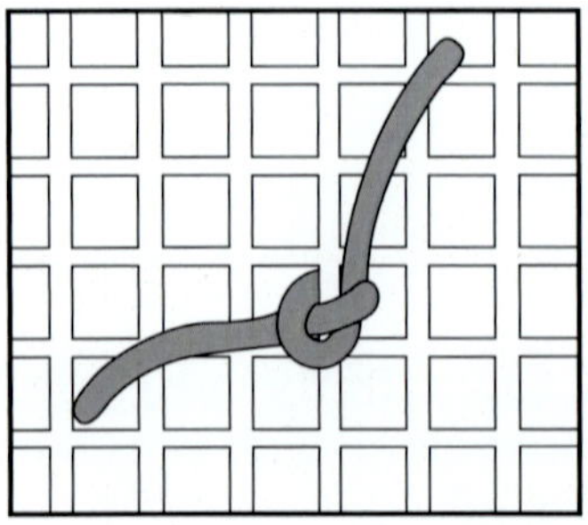

Top (32 x 32 threads)

KEY

COLOR (NL)	COLOR (NL)
white (41) - 17 yds	grey (38) - 12 yds
lt yellow (39) - 20 yds	black (00) Fr. knot - 1 yd
gold (11) - 3 yds	
red (02) - 5 yds	**COLOR (FLOSS)**
dk red (03) - 17 yds	*white - 18 yds
lt green (23) - 40 yds	*white Fr. knot
lt rust (10) - 12 yds	*Use 6 strands of floss.
brown (15) - 14 yds	

Side #1 (32 x 38 threads) (stitch 2)

Side #2 (32 x 38 threads) (stitch 2)

BALLET SCHOOL

Size: 4 1/2"w x 5 1/2"h x 4 1/2"d
(Fits a 4 1/4"w x 5 1/4"h x 4 1/4"d boutique tissue box.)
Supplies: Worsted weight yarn and metallic embroidery floss (refer to color key), two 10 1/2" x 13 1/2" sheets of clear 7 mesh plastic canvas, #16 tapestry needle, white tulle, and white sewing thread and needle.
Instructions:
1. Follow charts to cut and stitch tissue box cover pieces, working backstitches and Turkey loops last.
2. Using white overcast stitches, join Sides along long edges. Join Top to Sides.
3. For each tutu, cut three 14" x 3" pieces of tulle. Referring to Diagram, stack and gather tulle at top edge. Insert gathered section into hole on Side. Glue in place and trim edges.

Diagram

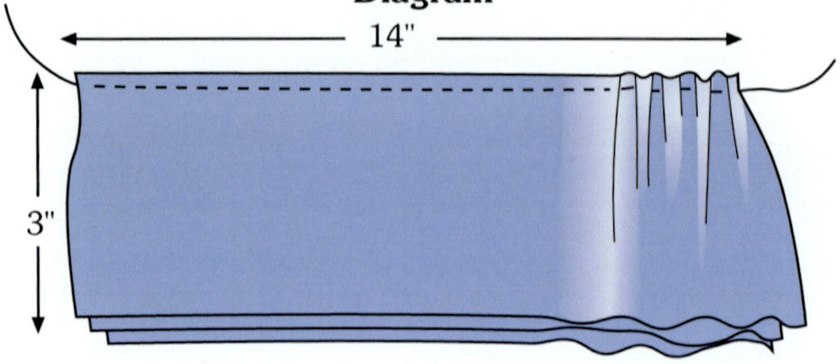

Top (32 x 32 threads)

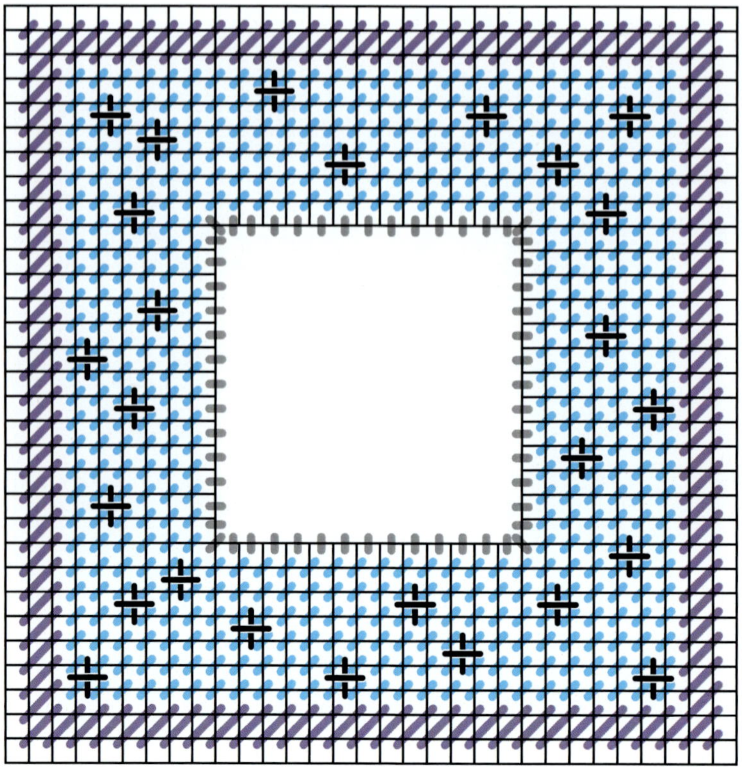

KEY

COLOR (YARN)	COLOR (YARN)
white - 20 yds	*green
flesh - 6 yds	*tan - 1 yd
lt pink - 17 yds	yellow Turkey loop - 5 yds
pink - 3 yds	brown Turkey loop
blue - 45 yds	*Use 2 plies of yarn.
green - 3 yds	COLOR (FLOSS)
brown - 5 yds	†metallic silver - 7 yds
black - 1 yd	†Use 6 strands of floss.
*pink	

Side #1 (32 x 38 threads) (stitch 2)

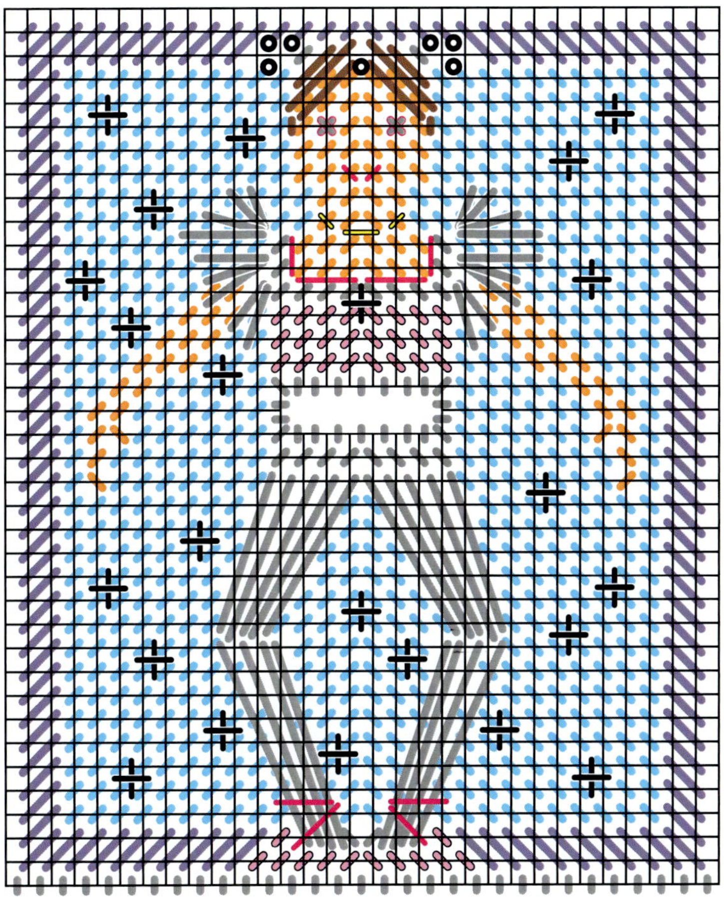

Side #2 (32 x 38 threads) (stitch 2)

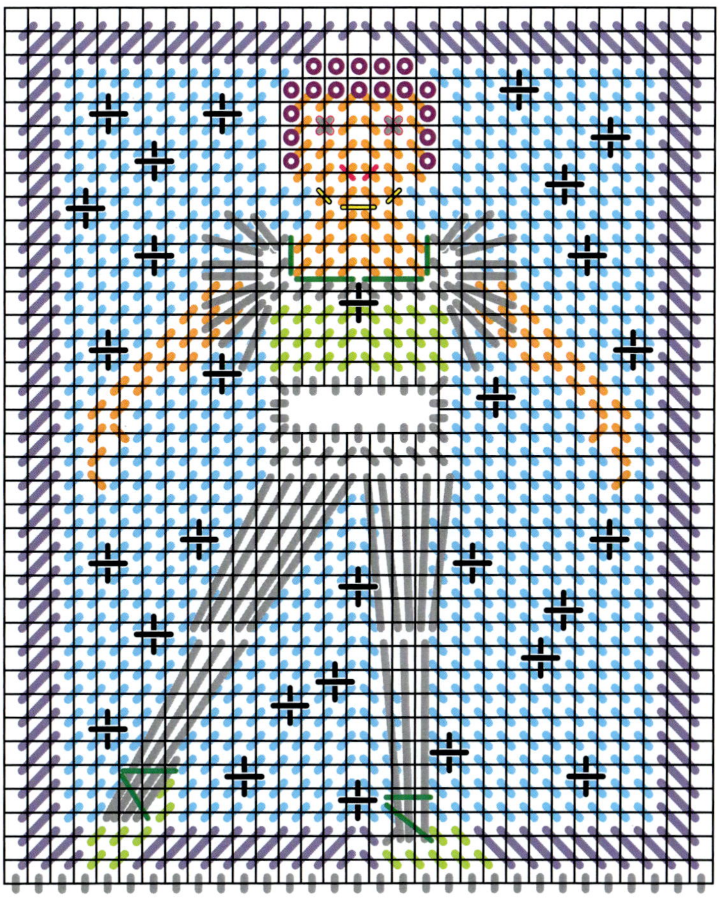

SPINNAKER

Size: 4 1/2"w x 5 1/2"h x 4 1/2"d
(*Fits a 4 1/4"w x 5 1/4"h x 4 1/4"d boutique tissue box.*)
Supplies: Worsted weight yarn and embroidery floss (refer to color key), two 10 1/2" x 13 1/2" sheets of clear 7 mesh plastic canvas, and #16 tapestry needle.
Instructions:
1. Follow charts to cut and stitch tissue box cover pieces, working backstitches last.
2. Using matching color overcast stitches, join Sides along long edges. Join Top to Sides.
3. For each Sail, match ♥'s, ★'s, and ♦'s, and tack corners of Sail to Side #1.

Sail (24 x 28 threads) (stitch 2)

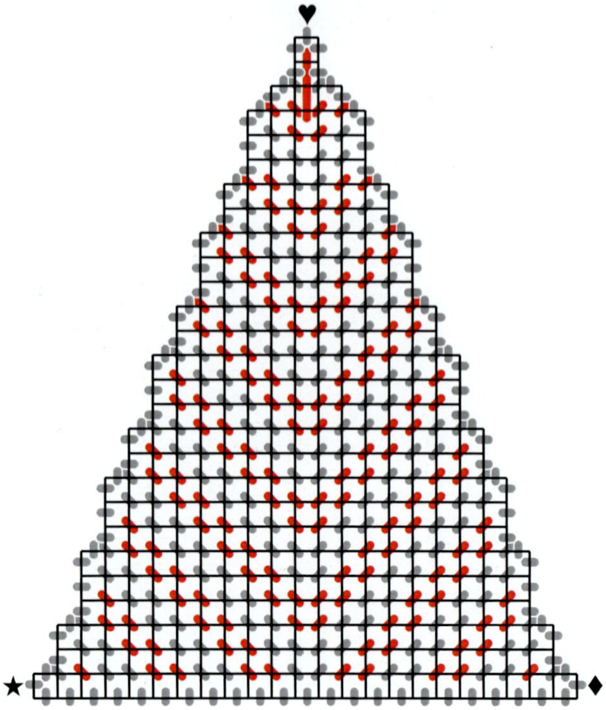

Top (32 x 32 threads)

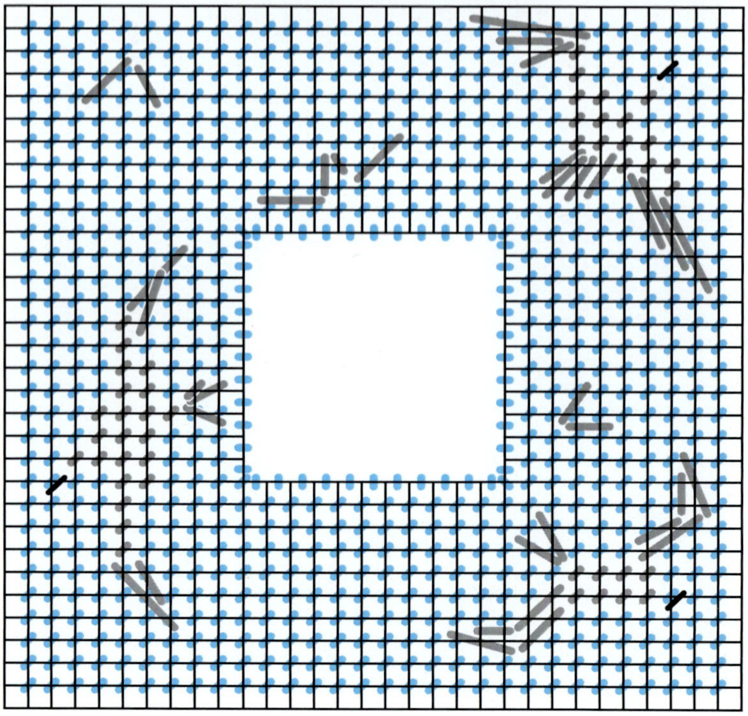

KEY

COLOR (YARN)	COLOR (FLOSS)
white - 32 yds	†white - 2 yds
yellow - 2 yds	♥black - 1 yd
red - 7 yds	†metallic silver - 6 yds
lt blue - 39 yds	†Use 6 strands of floss.
dk blue - 28 yds	♥Use 2 strands of floss.
green - 7 yds	
*red	

*Use 2 plies of yarn.

Side #1 (32 x 38 threads) (stitch 2)

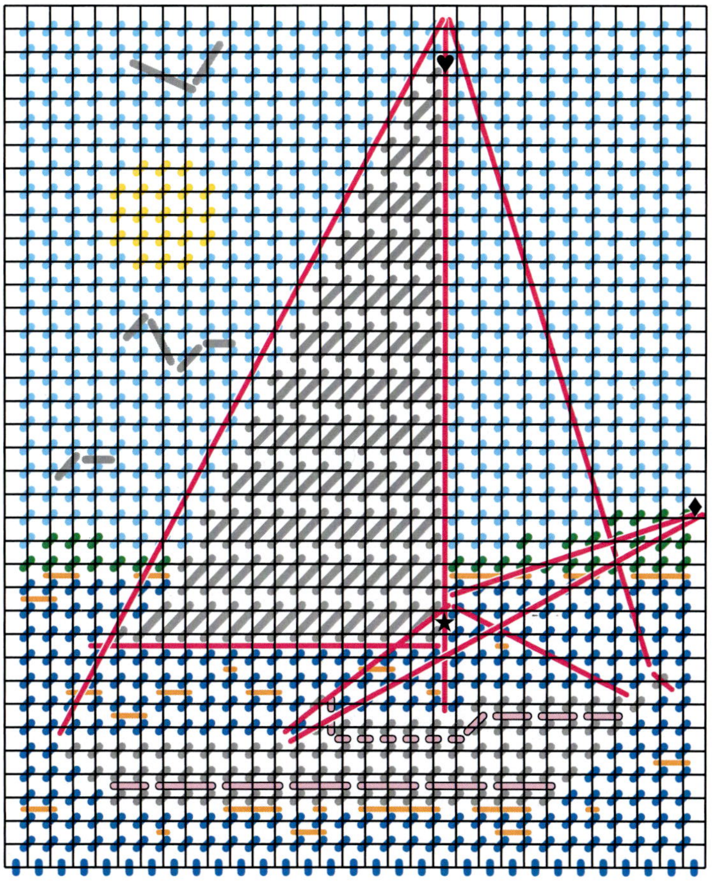

Side #2 (32 x 38 threads) (stitch 2)

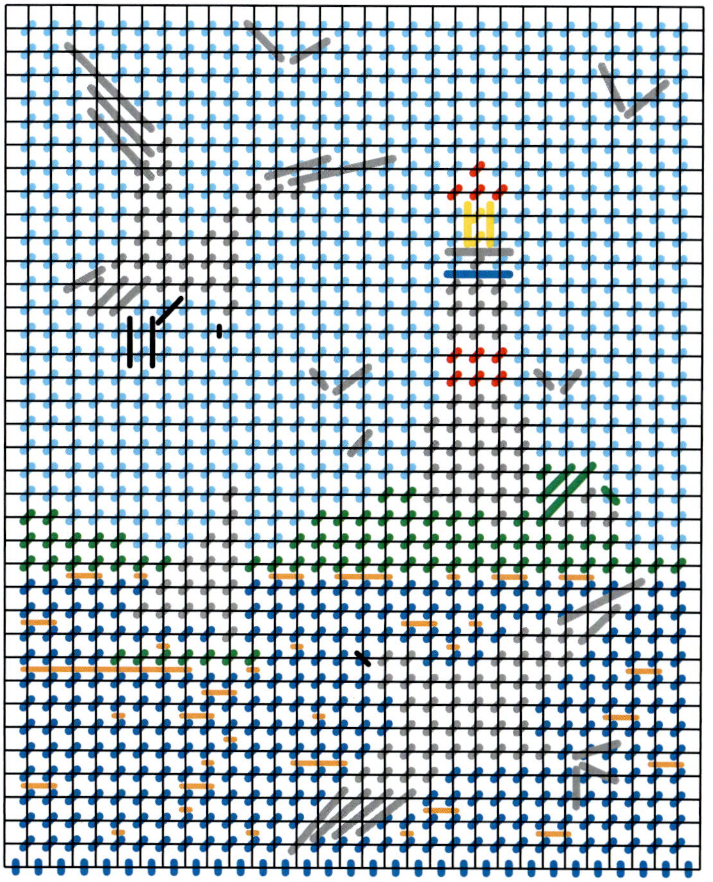

HOME SWEET HOME

Size: 4 1/2"w x 5 1/2"h x 4 1/2"d
(Fits a 4 1/4"w x 5 1/4"h x 4 1/4"d boutique tissue box.)
Supplies: Needloft® Plastic Canvas Yarn and embroidery floss (refer to color key), two 10 1/2" x 13 1/2" sheets of clear 7 mesh plastic canvas, and #16 tapestry needle.
Instructions:
1. Follow charts to cut and stitch tissue box cover pieces, working backstitches last.
2. Using lt blue overcast stitches, join Sides along long edges. Join Top to Sides.

KEY

COLOR (NL)
white (41) - 8 yds
yellow (19) - 4 yds
dk red (42) - 22 yds
lt blue (35) - 56 yds
green (27) - 25 yds
black (00) - 8 yds
COLOR (FLOSS)
*white - 3 yds
*brown - 2 yds
†black - 8 yds
*black

*Use 6 strands of floss.
†Use 2 strands of floss.

Side (32 x 38 threads) (stitch 4)

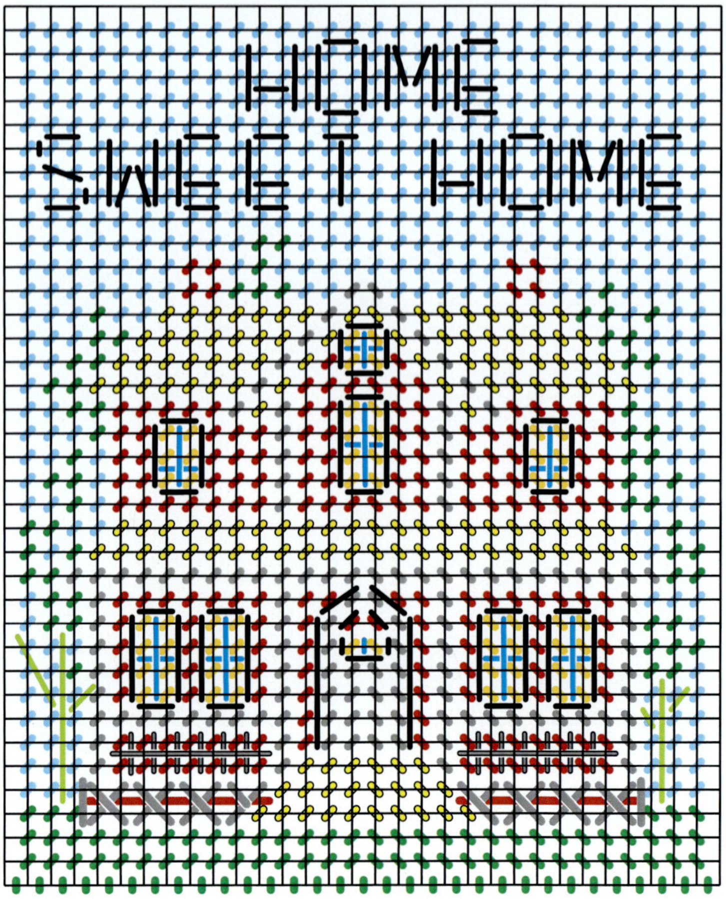

Top (32 x 32 threads)

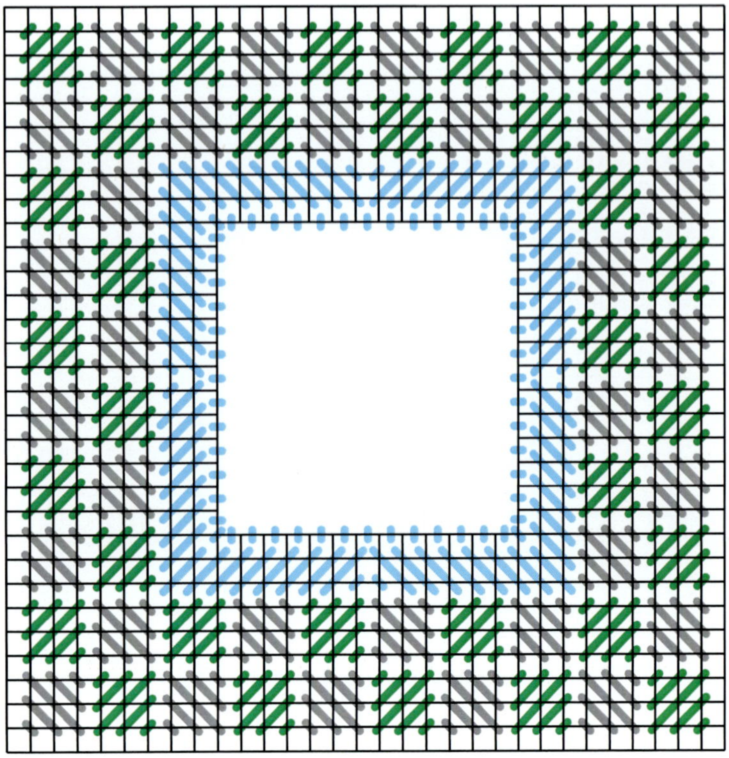

WELCOME

Size: 4$^{1}/_{2}$"w x 5$^{1}/_{2}$"h x 4$^{1}/_{2}$"d
(Fits a 4¼"w x 5¼"h x 4¼"d boutique tissue box.)
Supplies: Needloft® Plastic Canvas Yarn and embroidery floss (refer to color key), two 10$^{1}/_{2}$" x 13$^{1}/_{2}$" sheets of clear 7 mesh plastic canvas, and #16 tapestry needle.
Instructions:
1. Follow charts to cut and stitch tissue box cover pieces, working backstitches last.
2. Using lt yellow overcast stitches, join Sides along long edges. Join Top to Sides.

KEY

COLOR (NL)
- lt yellow (39) - 56 yds
- green (27) - 25 yds
- rust (12) - 29 yds

COLOR (FLOSS)
- *green - 23 yds

*Use 6 strands of floss.

Side (32 x 38 threads) (stitch 4)

Top (32 x 32 threads)

NURSERY

Size: 4 1/2"w x 5 1/2"h x 4 1/2"d
(Fits a 4 1/4"w x 5 1/4"h x 4 1/4"d boutique tissue box.)
Supplies: Worsted weight yarn and embroidery floss (refer to color key), two 10 1/2" x 13 1/2" sheets of clear 7 mesh plastic canvas, #16 tapestry needle, and four 21" lengths of white ribbon.
Instructions:
1. Follow charts to cut and stitch tissue box cover pieces, working backstitches and French knots last.
2. Using lt blue overcast stitches, join Sides along long edges. Join Top to Sides.
3. For each bow, thread white ribbon through holes on Side. Tie bow and trim ends.

Top (30 x 30 threads)

KEY

COLOR (YARN)	COLOR (YARN)
white - 12 yds	*lt blue
lt yellow - 8 yds	*Use 2 plies of yarn.
lt pink - 13 yds	
pink - 10 yds	COLOR (FLOSS)
lt blue - 32 yds	†black - 2 yds
lt green - 8 yds	♥black Fr. knot
tan - 3 yds	†Use 2 strands of floss.
brown - 13 yds	♥Use 6 strands of floss.

Side #1 (30 x 38 threads) (stitch 2)

Side #2 (30 x 38 threads) (stitch 2)

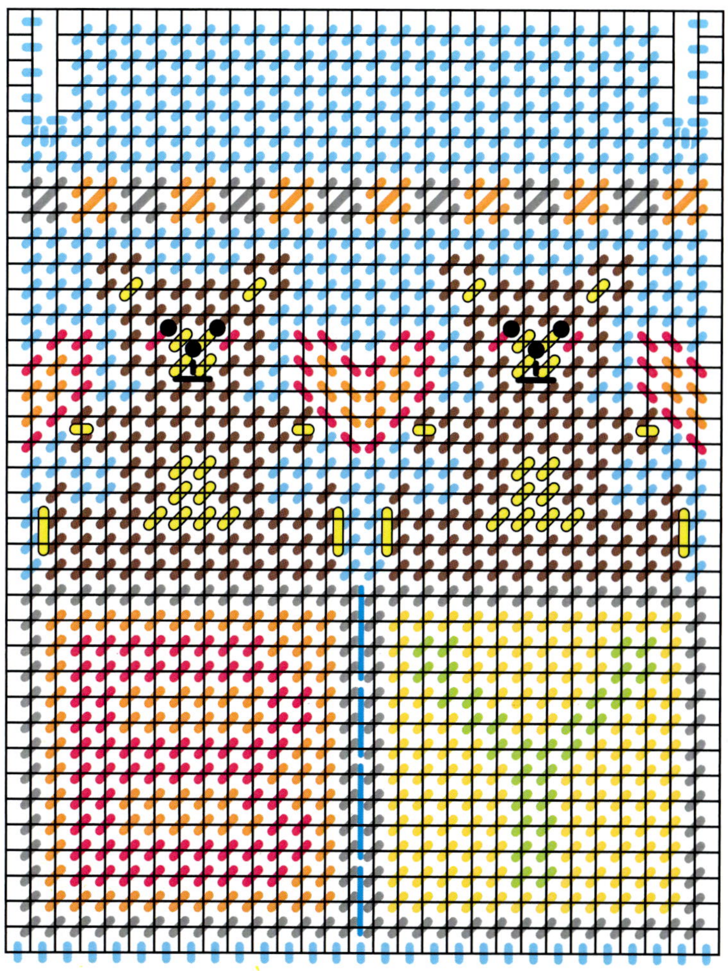

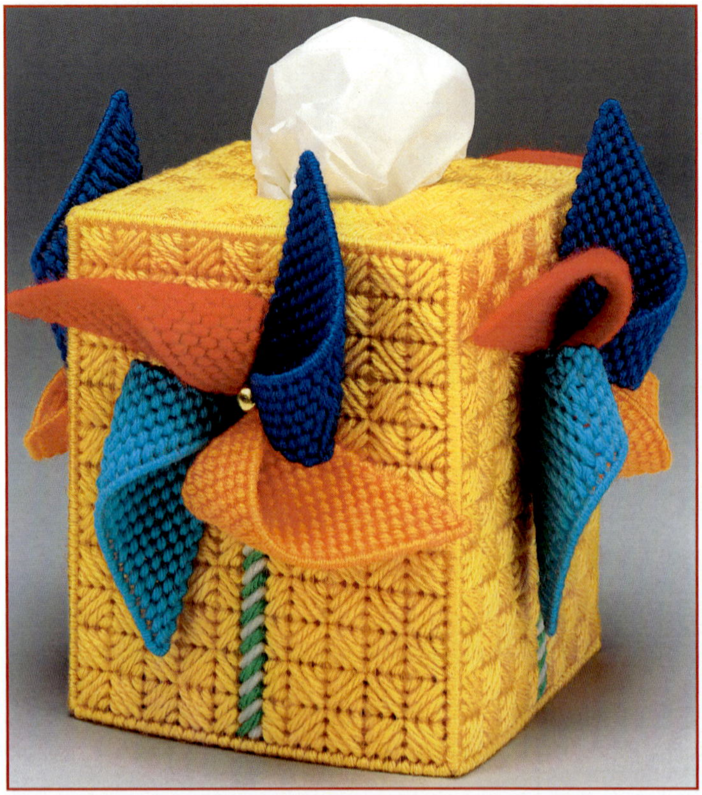

PASTEL & BRIGHT PINWHEELS

Size: 4 1/2"w x 5 1/2"h x 4 1/2"d
(Fits a 4 1/4"w x 5 1/4"h x 4 1/4"d boutique tissue box.)
Supplies: Worsted weight yarn (refer to color key), three 10 1/2" x 13 1/2" sheets of clear 7 mesh plastic canvas, #16 tapestry needle, and four 3/4" paper fasteners.
Instructions:
1. Referring to photo and color keys for yarn colors, follow charts to cut and stitch tissue box cover pieces, leaving grey shaded areas unworked.
2. Using matching color overcast stitches, join Sides along long edges. Join Top to Sides.
3. For each Pinwheel, turn Pinwheel piece over. Work stitches in grey shaded areas on "wrong side" of Pinwheel. With "right side" up, fold indicated corners of Pinwheel to center and tack. Insert paper fastener in Pinwheel and Side at ♥. Secure fastener on inside of tissue box cover.

Pinwheel (30 x 30 threads) (stitch 4)

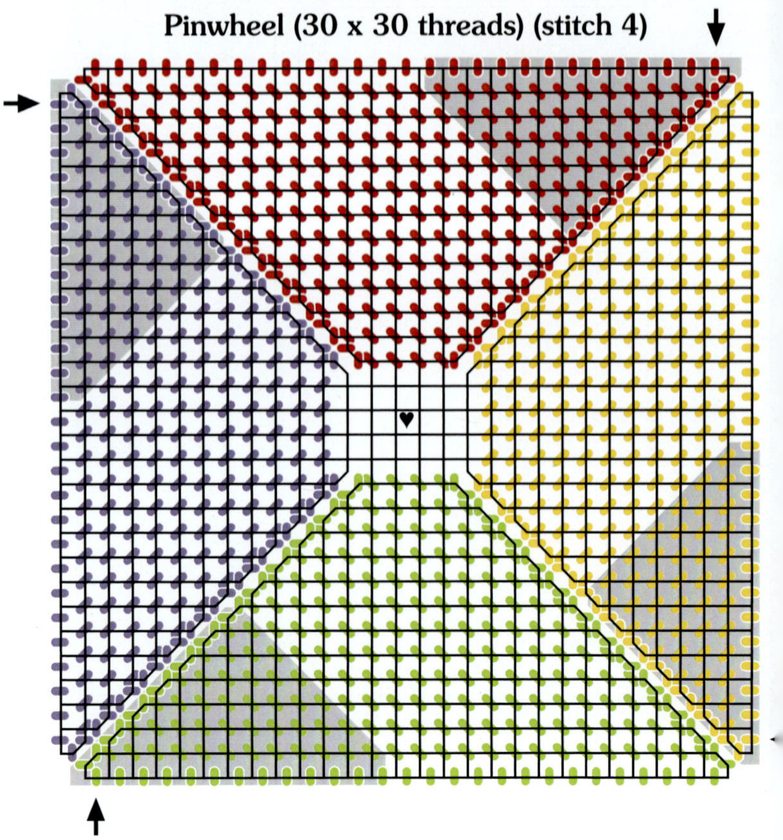

PASTEL KEY

COLOR (YARN)
white - 3 yds
lt yellow - 20 yds
lt pink - 20 yds
lt purple - 20 yds
purple - 2 yds
lt blue - 70 yds
lt green - 20 yds

BRIGHT KEY

COLOR (YARN)
white - 3 yds
yellow - 70 yds
orange - 20 yds
red - 20 yds
green - 2 yds
dk blue - 20 yds
turquoise - 20 yds

Side (32 x 38 threads) (stitch 4)

Top (32 x 32 threads)

FLEUR-DE-LIS

Size: 4 1/2"w x 5 1/2"h x 4 1/2"d
(Fits a 4 1/4"w x 5 1/4"h x 4 1/4"d boutique tissue box.)
Supplies: Worsted weight yarn and Rainbow Gallery metallic yarn (refer to color key), two 10 1/2" x 13 1/2" sheets of clear 7 mesh plastic canvas, and #16 tapestry needle.
Instructions:
1. Follow charts to cut and stitch tissue box cover pieces, working backstitches last and leaving grey shaded areas unworked.
2. Work stitches in grey shaded areas to join Sides along long edges.
3. Using ecru overcast stitches, join remaining unworked edges of Sides along long edges. Join Top to Sides.

KEY

COLOR (YARN)
- ecru - 51 yds
- metallic gold - 32 yds

Side (32 x 38 threads) (stitch 4)

Top (32 x 32 threads)

PLASTIC CANVAS BASICS

WORKING WITH PLASTIC CANVAS

Counting Threads. Throughout this leaflet, the lines of the canvas will be referred to as threads. However, they are not actually "threads" since the canvas is not woven. Before cutting out your pieces, note the thread count of each chart. The thread count is listed above the chart and indicates the number of threads in the width and height of the canvas pieces. To cut plastic canvas pieces accurately, count **threads** (not **holes**) as shown in **Fig. 1**.

Fig. 1

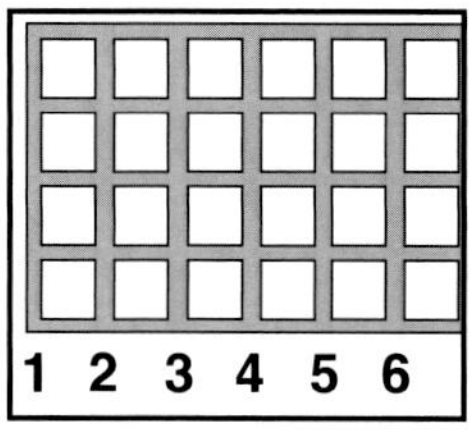

Marking the Canvas. If you find it necessary to mark on the canvas, use an overhead projector pen. Outline shape with pen, cut out shape, and remove markings with water and a towel.

Cutting the Canvas. When cutting canvas, make sure to cut as close to the thread as possible without cutting into the thread. If you don't cut close enough, "nubs" or "pickets" will be left on the edge of your canvas. Make sure to cut off all nubs from the canvas before you begin to stitch, because nubs will snag the yarn or floss and are difficult to cover.

WORKING WITH YARN AND FLOSS

Selecting Yarn And Floss. We used various brands of worsted weight yarn, Needloft® Plastic Canvas Yarn, and embroidery floss to stitch the photography models for this leaflet.

Separating Yarn Strands. Most brands of worsted weight yarn have four plies that are twisted together to form one strand. When the instructions say to use two plies of yarn, simply remove two plies of the yarn and stitch with the remaining two plies. Needloft yarn cannot be separated; use six strands of embroidery floss in place of two plies of yarn.

Separating Floss Strands. Embroidery floss consists of six strands that are twisted together. To ensure smoother stitches, separate the strands of floss and realign them before threading needle.

Dye Lot Variations. It is important to buy all of the yarn or floss you need to complete your project from the same dye lot. Although variations in color may be slight when yarns or flosses from two different dye lots are held together, the variation is usually apparent on a stitched piece.

READING THE COLOR KEY

A color key is included for each project. The heading in each color key is for the descriptive color name (**COLOR**), worsted weight yarn (**YARN**), Needloft yarn (**NL**), Paternayan Persian Yarn (**PERSIAN**), or embroidery floss (**FLOSS**). The key indicates the colors of yarn or floss used and how each color is represented on the chart. For example, when white yarn is represented by a grey line in the color key, all grey stitches on the chart should be stitched using white yarn.

READING THE CHART

Whenever possible, the drawing on the chart looks like the completed stitch. For example, the tent stitches on the chart are drawn diagonally across one intersection of threads just like tent stitches look on your piece of canvas. Likewise, Gobelin stitches on the chart look identical to the Gobelin stitches on your canvas. When a stitch cannot clearly be drawn on the chart, like a French knot, a symbol will be used instead. If you have difficulty determining how a particular stitch is worked, refer to Stitch Diagrams, pg. 22.

STITCHING THE DESIGN

Securing the First Stitch. Don't knot the end of your yarn or floss before you begin stitching. Instead, begin each length of yarn or floss by coming up from the wrong side of the canvas and leaving a 1" - 2" tail on the wrong side. Hold this tail against the canvas and work the first few stitches over the tail. When secure, clip the tail close to your stitched piece. Clipping the tail closely is important because long tails can become tangled in future stitches or can show through to the right side of the canvas.

Using Even Tension. Keep your stitching tension consistent, with each stitch lying flat and even on the canvas. Pulling or yanking the yarn or floss causes the tension to be too tight, and you will be able to see through your project. Loose tension is caused by not pulling the yarn or floss firmly enough, and the yarn or floss will not lie flat on the canvas.

Ending Your Stitches. After you've completed all of the stitches of one color in an area, end your stitching by running your needle under several stitches on the back of the stitched piece. To keep the tails of the yarn or floss from showing through or becoming tangled in future stitches, trim the end of the yarn or floss close to the stitched piece.

Stitching Tips

Length of Yarn or Floss. It is best to begin stitching with a piece of yarn or floss that is approximately one yard long. However, when working large areas of the same color, you may want to begin with a longer length of yarn or floss to reduce the number of ends and keep the back of your project looking neat.

Keeping Stitches Smooth. Most stitches tend to twist the yarn or floss. Drop your needle and let the yarn or floss untwist every few stitches or whenever needed.

JOINING PIECES

Straight Edges. The most common method of assembling stitched pieces is joining two or more pieces of canvas along a straight edge using overcast stitches. Place one piece on top of the other with right or wrong sides together. Make sure the edges being joined are even, then stitch the pieces together through all layers.

Shaded Areas. The shaded area is part of a chart that has colored shading on top of it. Shaded areas usually mean that all the stitches in that area are used to join pieces of canvas. Do not work the stitches in a shaded area until your project instructions say you should.

Tacking. To tack pieces, run your needle under the backs of some stitches on one stitched piece to secure the yarn or floss. Then run your needle through the canvas or under the stitches on the piece to be tacked in place. The idea is to securely attach your pieces without your tacking stitches showing.

STITCH DIAGRAMS

Bring threaded needle up at 1 and all odd numbers and down at 2 and all even numbers.

TENT STITCH

This stitch is worked in horizontal or vertical rows over one intersection as shown in **Fig. 2**. Refer to **Fig. 3** to work the reversed tent stitch.

Fig. 2

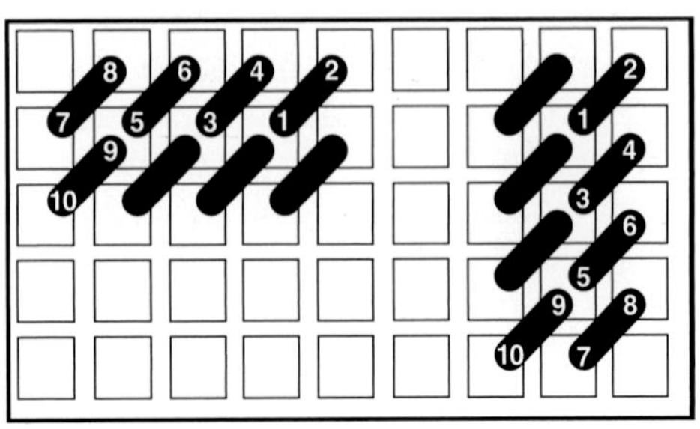

Fig. 3

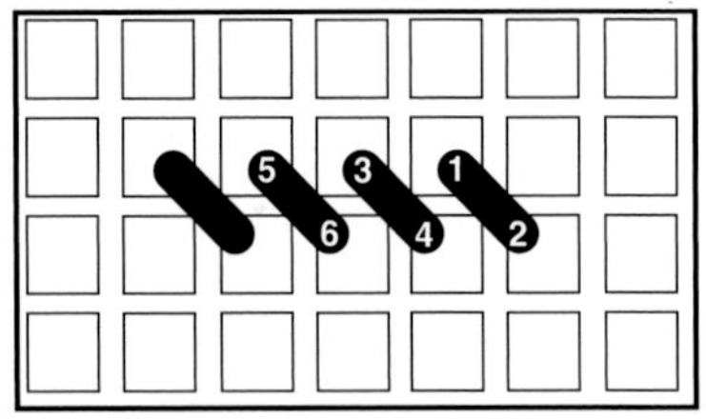

GOBELIN STITCH

This basic straight stitch is worked over two or more threads or intersections (**Fig. 4**). The number of threads or intersections may vary according to the chart.

Fig. 4

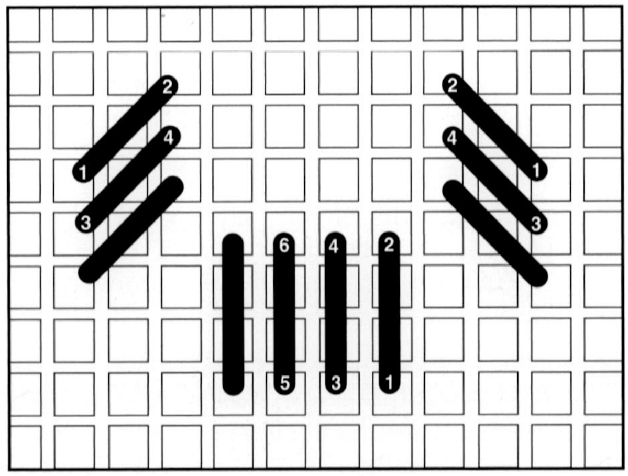

ALTERNATING SCOTCH STITCH

This Scotch stitch variation is worked over a number of threads forming alternating blocks as shown in **Fig. 5**.

Fig. 5

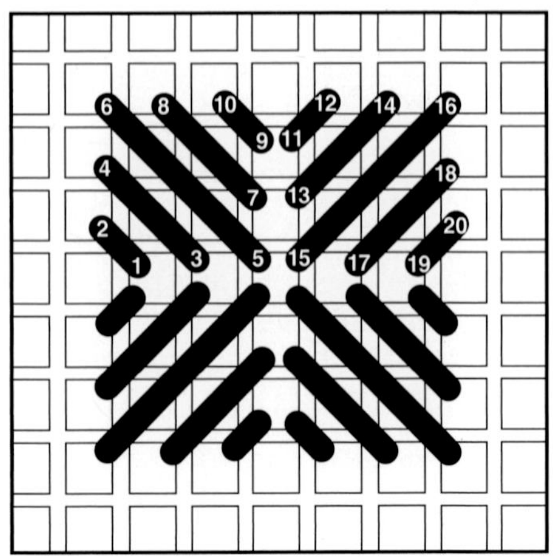

MOSAIC STITCH

This three-stitch pattern forms small squares (**Fig. 6**).

Fig. 6

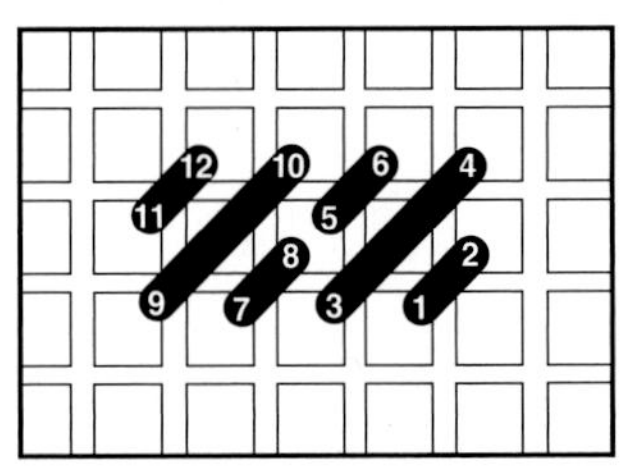

CROSS STITCH

This stitch is composed of two stitches (**Fig. 7**). The top stitch of each cross must always be made in the same direction.

Fig. 7

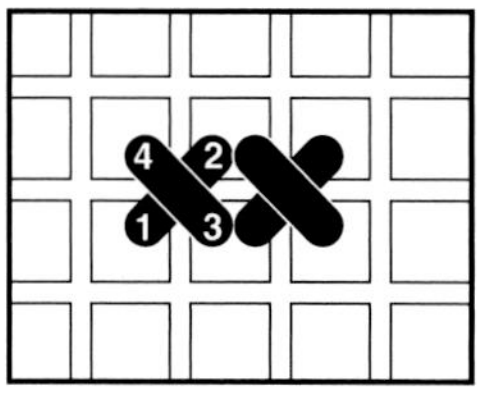

UPRIGHT CROSS STITCH

This stitch is worked over two threads as shown in **Fig. 8**. The top stitch of each cross must always be made in the same direction.

Fig. 8

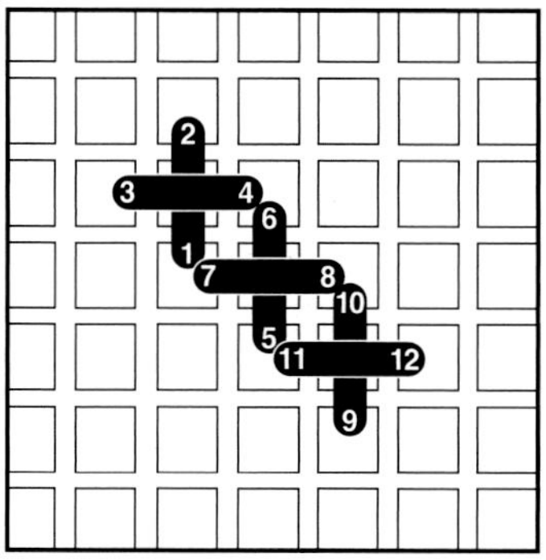

BACKSTITCH

This stitch is worked over completed stitches to outline or define (**Fig. 9**). It is sometimes worked over more than one thread.

Fig. 9

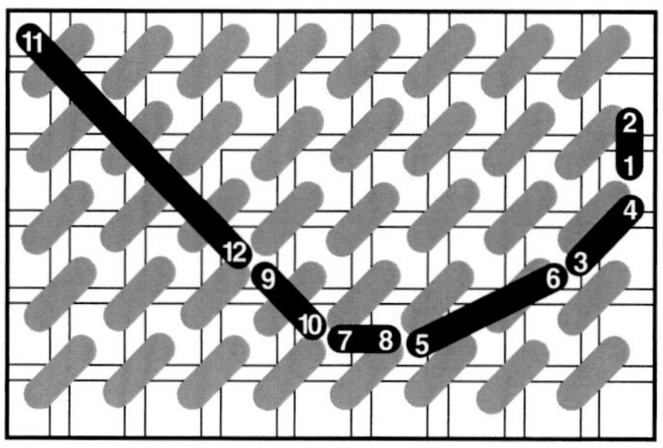

FRENCH KNOT

Come up at 1. Wrap yarn or floss once around needle. Insert the needle at 2 and pull it through the canvas, holding the yarn or floss until it must be released (**Fig. 10**).

Fig. 10

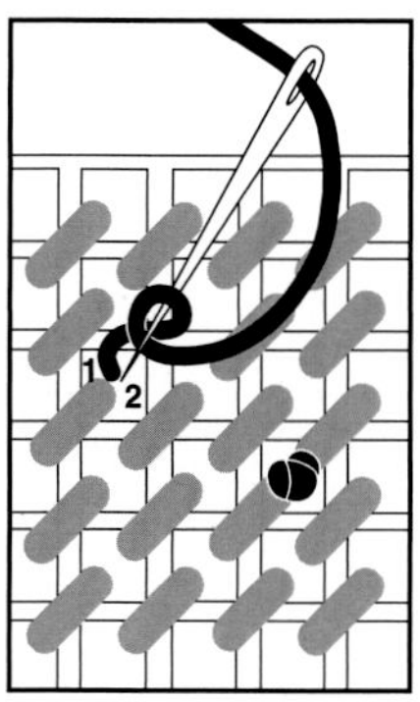

DOUBLE FRENCH KNOT

Bring needle up through hole. Wrap yarn twice around needle and insert needle in same hole, holding end of yarn with non-stitching fingers (**Fig. 11**). Tighten knot; then pull needle through canvas, holding yarn until it must be released.

Fig. 11

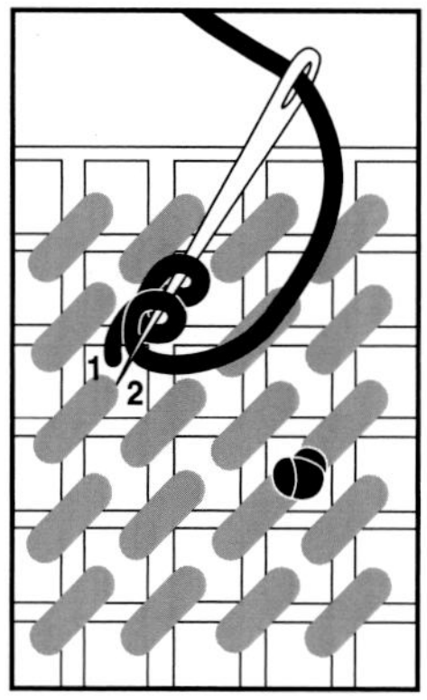

TURKEY LOOP STITCH

This stitch is composed of locked loops. Bring needle up through hole and back down through same hole, forming a loop on top of the canvas. A locking stitch is then made across the thread directly below or to either side of the loop as shown in **Fig. 12**.

Fig. 12

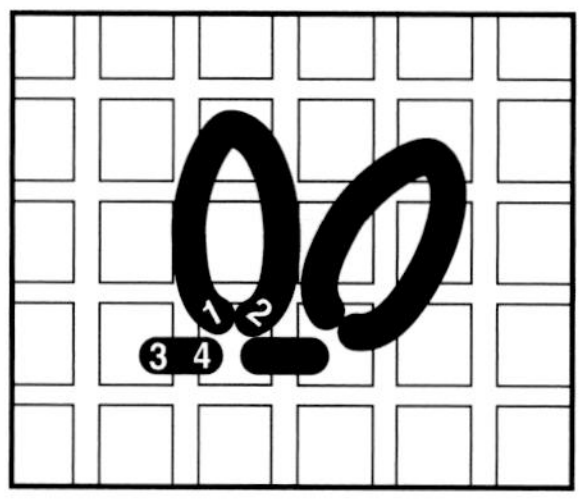

OVERCAST STITCH

This stitch covers the edge of the canvas and joins pieces of canvas (**Fig. 13**). It may be necessary to go through the same hole more than once to get even coverage on the edge, especially at the corners.

Fig. 13

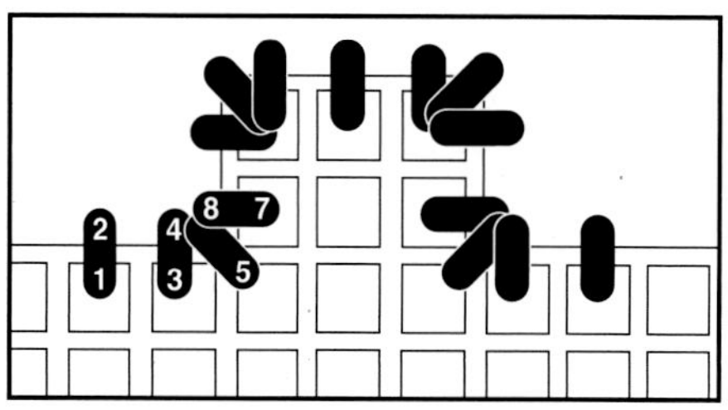

Show us what you're working on!

Share your project photos with us on social media.
Tag us @leisureartsinc or use #leisurearts

Made in U.S.A.

Instructions tested and some cover items made by Kandi Ashford, Mary Kennemur, and Linda Rogers-Peters.

Production Team: Writer – Merrilee Gasaway; Artist – John Rose; and Photo Stylist – Tiffany Huffman.

We have made every effort to ensure that these instructions are accurate and complete. We cannot, however, be responsible for human error, typographical mistakes, or variations in individual work.